Progressive
Classical Guitar
Method for Young Beginners
Book 1

by Connie Bull

Illustrated by James and Hazel Stewart

PROGRESSIVE CLASSICAL GUITAR METHOD FOR YOUNG BEGINNERS BOOK 1
I.S.B.N. 978 1 86469 206 8
Order Code: CP-69206
For more information on this series contact;
LTP Publishing Pty Ltd
email: info@learntoplaymusic.com
or visit our website;
www.learntoplaymusic.com

Published by
**KOALA MUSIC
PUBLICATIONS**

Introduction

The *Progressive Classical Guitar Method for Young Beginners book 1* is designed to teach the young beginner guitar with a classical approach right from the beginning. The student will learn correct posture, how to hold the guitar, right and left hand positions and the rest stroke. Six notes on the first and second string are introduced, along with over 20 pieces to help introduce material from preliminary grade theory such as note values, rests, time signatures, the lead-in and even an introduction to composition.

Let's Practice Together

It is important to have the correct practice method right from the beginning. You should practice every day if possible for 10 minutes at the beginning (later you can increase your practice time to 20 or 30 minutes once your fingers are more flexible and used to the strings), rather than only once or twice a week. Always practice small portions at a time before moving on to new things and start slowly. When practicing a new piece, take it a bar at a time and always count aloud, until you can play along with the CD without stopping.

We have recorded all the songs in this book onto a CD. When your teacher's not there, instead of practicing by yourself, you can play along with us. Practicing will be much more fun and you will learn faster.

- Woodblock clicks are used to begin each exercise.

- At the beginning of the CD there are **six** tuning notes – **E, A, D, G, B**, and **E**, which correspond to the **open strings** of the guitar. It is a good idea to tune the guitar to these notes before every practice session. Tuning is difficult at first, so it is best to have your teacher tune your guitar whenever possible. In time, you will be able to do it yourself.

 **1   Tuning Notes - E, A, D, G, B, E.**

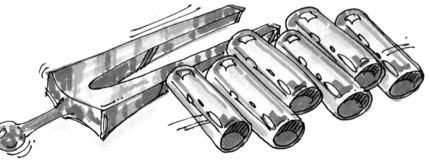

Contents

How to Hold the Guitar

Look at the following picture and check if you are holding your guitar in the correct position. If you do not have a footstool, some phone books stacked on top of each other will do until you can use a footstool.

This position might be uncomfortable for a little while. While you're getting used to the position, remember the following things:

• keep the tuning keys level with your eyes.

• sit forward on the tip of the chair (use a chair without arm rests).

• Make sure that the bottom indented part of the guitar body rests flat on your left leg.

A music stand is also recommended, but a high table or desk or paper stand can be used as a substitute at first if necessary.

Parts of the Guitar

Trace the outline of the guitar.

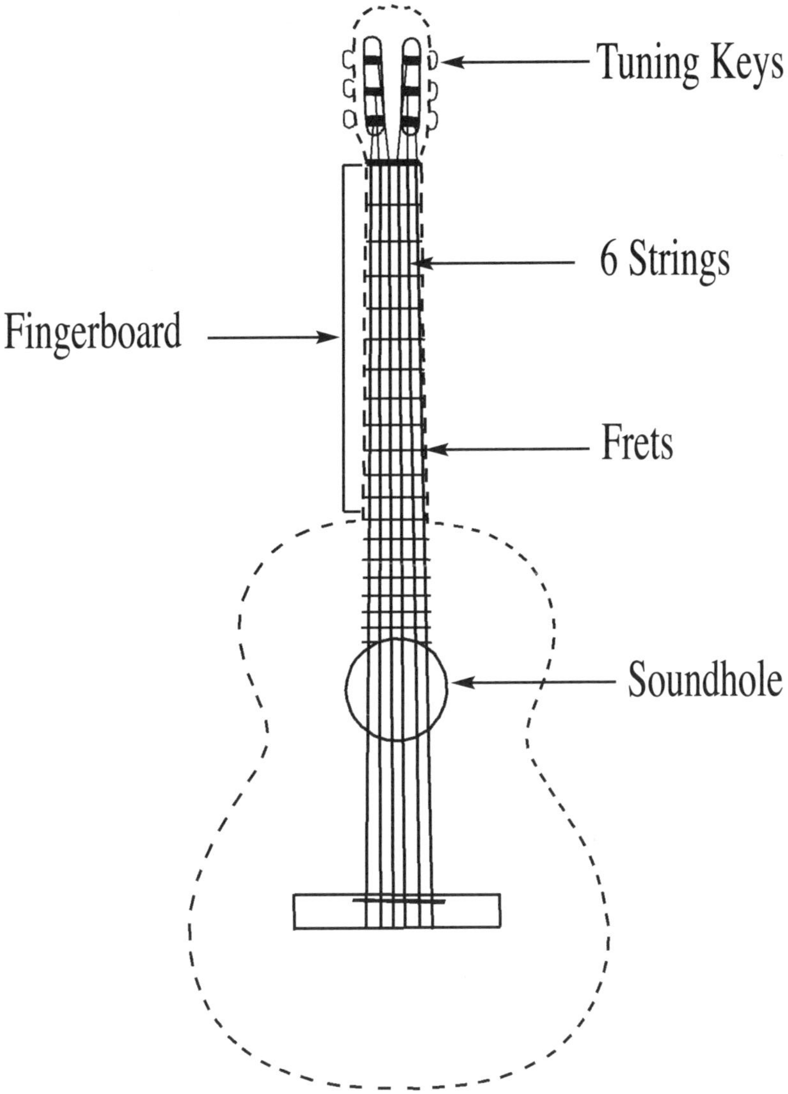

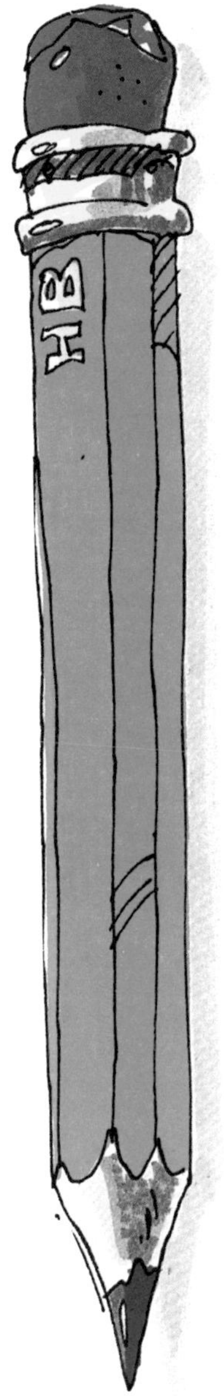

Write down the correct names for each part of the guitar

Tuning Keys

6 Strings

Fingerboard

Frets

Soundhole

Point to your own guitar, naming the parts aloud.

The Strings

The strings of the guitar have letter names. They are: **E**, **A**, **D**, **G**, **B** and **E**. Trace the letter names.

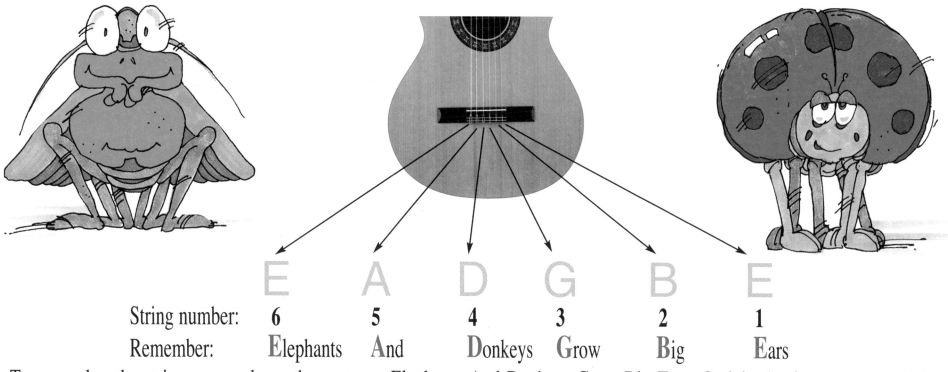

String number:	**6**	**5**	**4**	**3**	**2**	**1**
Remember:	**E**lephants	**A**nd	**D**onkeys	**G**row	**B**ig	**E**ars

To remember the string names, learn the sentence Elephants And Donkeys Grow Big Ears. Or join the four sentences below by connecting the correct type of lines, then write down the sentences in the correct order. Memorize the one you like best to remember the order of the strings of the guitar.

Eggs	Ants	Dad	Goes	Bananas	Eventually
Every	And	Devours	Go	Blocks	Eventually
Eleven	Afternoon	Drag	Green	Brown	Entirely
Every	Ape	Dates	Giant	Berserk	Easily

The Right Hand

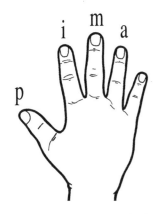

The letter names for the right hand are: **p-i-m-a**.

Trace your own right hand into the box and put the correct letter names above it.

Remember the letters by using this sentence:
Practicing **i**s **m**y **a**im.
Copy this sentence: _____

Lesson 1

Position of the Right Hand

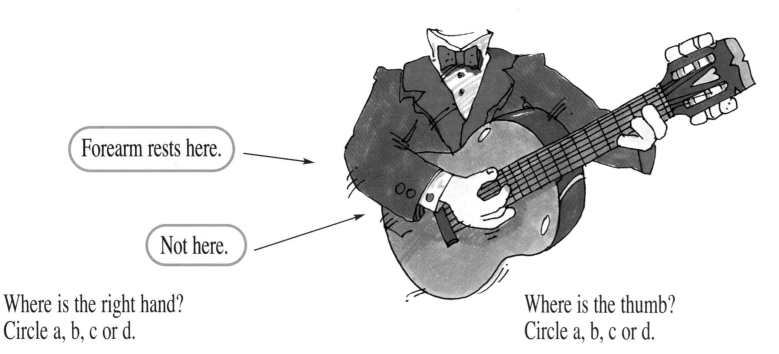

Forearm rests here.

Not here.

Where is the right hand?
Circle a, b, c or d.

a. Over the fingerboard.
b. Over the soundhole.
c. Behind the guitar.
d. On the teacher's guitar.

Practice the correct right hand position.

Where is the thumb?
Circle a, b, c or d.

a. Behind the strings.
b. In the air.
c. On the frets.
d. Resting on the sixth string.

Practice the correct thumb position.

The Rest Stroke

Go for a walk around the room. Look carefully at how your legs move, one and then the other. Now do the same with your fingers "i" and "m" on your knee. Do it slowly and watch how when one finger is in front, the other goes to the back.
This style is used for our **rest stroke**, called **alternating**.

With your thumb resting correctly, place your "i" finger on string number one (E string) as indicated below.

Pull the finger across, using the tip of the finger and let it come to rest on the second string.

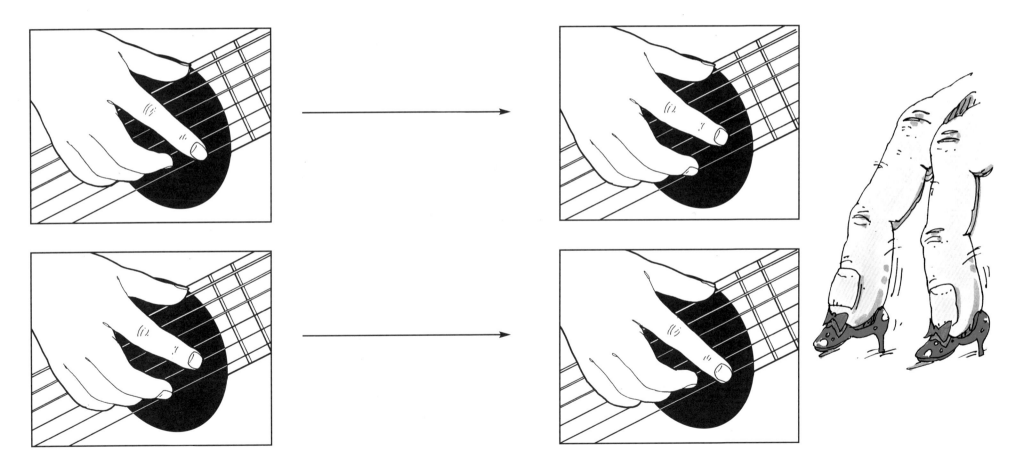

Now bring your "m" finger to the E string and pull it across to the second string. Like the "walking" discussed above, at the same time bring the "i" finger back to the first string.

The Open Strings

An **open string** is played by using the right hand only. Play these first pieces with the rest stroke, learned on the previous page. A **piece** is the word used for song in classical music. Remember, it's like walking with your fingers.

Play this on the open first string (**E**). Remember to rest your right thumb on the low E string (sixth string).

> **This double bar line shows the end of a piece.**

2   I'm E

> **Bar Line**

i m i m i m i m i m i m i m i m i m i m

bar   bar   bar   bar

Play this on the open second string (**B**).

3   I'm B

i m i m i m i m i m i m i m i m i m i m

Play this on the open third string (**G**)

4   I'm G

i m i m i m i m i m i m i m i m i m i m

Lesson 2
How to Read Music

Music Notes

Like the strings of the guitar, letters are used for music notes:

This is called the **musical alphabet**.

The Quarter Note

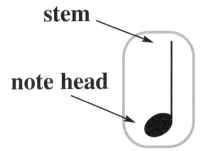

stem

note head

Count: 1

This is a musical note called a **quarter note** (or crotchet). It lasts for **one** beat or count.

Play the two exercises on this page on the second string (**B**) after you have completed the tracing. Remember to use **i** and **m** and to use the rest stroke.

Trace the quarter note stems going up, the barlines and the double bar line.

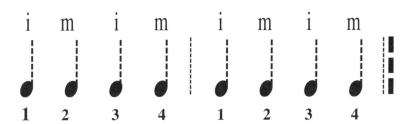

i   m   i   m   i   m   i   m

Count: 1   2   3   4   1   2   3   4

Draw your own stems going up and trace the barlines and the double bar line.

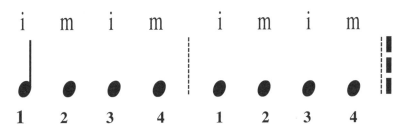

i   m   i   m   i   m   i   m

Count: 1   2   3   4   1   2   3   4

The Staff

These five lines are called the **staff** or **stave**.

Music notes are written in the spaces and on the lines of the staff.

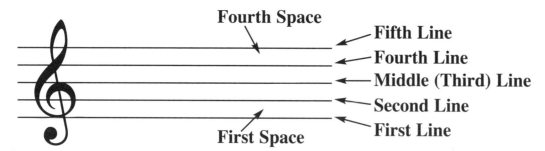

Fourth Space

Fifth Line
Fourth Line
Middle (Third) Line
Second Line
First Line

First Space

The Four Four Time Signature

These two numbers are called the **four four** time signature.
The 4/4 time signature tells you there are **four** beats in each bar.
There are **four** quarter notes in a bar of 4/4 time.

The Treble Clef

This is called a **treble clef.**
All classical guitar music has a treble clef at the beginning of each piece.

Trace the quarter notes in the spaces and lines and fill in the note heads.

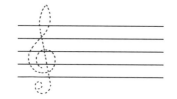

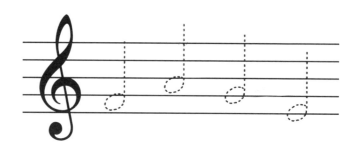

The 4/4 time signature is placed after the treble clef on the staff.

The Note E

So far all quarter note stems have pointed **up**. Quarter note stems can also go down, as with the **E** note shown below.

Is the note **E** in a space or on line?

_____

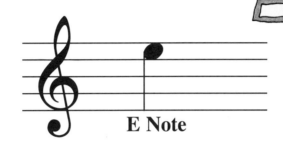

E Note

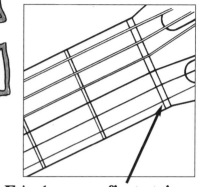

The note **E** is the **open first string**. No left hand fingers are used.

Play the following piece using the rest stroke. There are four quarter notes in each bar. Count aloud while playing. There are 4 beats on the recording to introduce this piece.

5   All Even

Repeat Sign

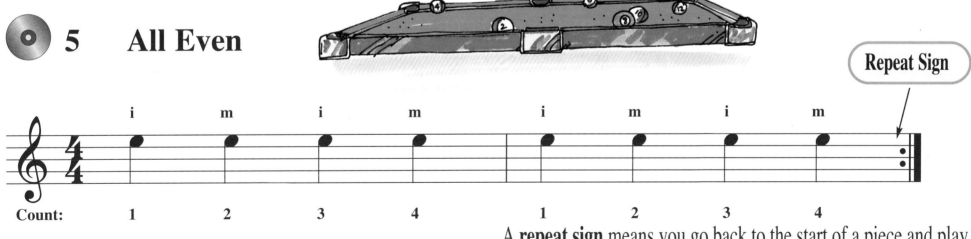

A **repeat sign** means you go back to the start of a piece and play again. How many times will you play a piece that has a repeat sign? _____

Lesson 3
The Left Hand

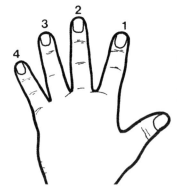

The hand fingers are numbered 1, 2, 3, 4.

Trace your own left hand into the box and put the correct numbers above it.

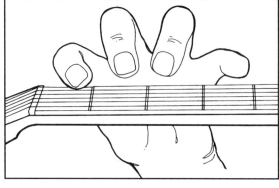

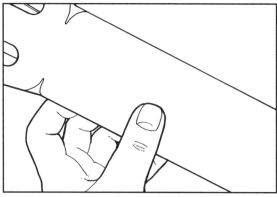

When using the left hand, the **tips** of the fingers are always used to play the strings and the finger should be **curved**. (It is important to keep the nails of this hand short). The fingers are placed **just behind the frets**, not in the middle of the frets. The thumb of your left hand is in the middle of the back of the neck.

The Note F

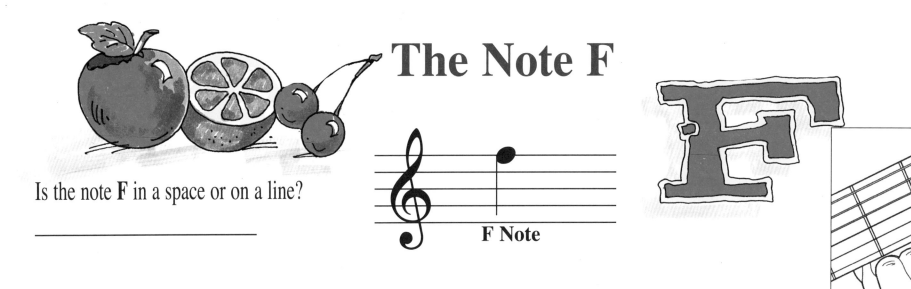

Is the note **F** in a space or on a line?

_____

F Note

Play this **F** note with your **first finger** behind the **first fret** on the **first string**.

Count aloud while playing the next piece. Curve your first finger and use the tip of the finger while playing the note **F**.

 6   **Fruit Piece**

The **F** note is **higher** on the staff than the E note and therefore will also **sound** higher.

E   F

Things to remember:
1. A new piece should always be played slowly and evenly.
2. Use i-m rest stroke, starting with the i finger and rest the thumb on the top string.
3. When not playing with the CD, always count 1, 2, 3, 4 before starting to establish an even tempo (= pace).

The Half Note

Count: 1 2

This is called a **half note** (or minim).
It lasts for **two** beats.
There are **two** half notes in one bar of $\frac{4}{4}$ time.

Trace these half notes, but do not fill in the note head.

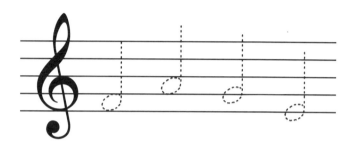

Clap and count the following exercises before playing. Remember to use the tip of your finger when playing **F**.

 7   Minimal Two

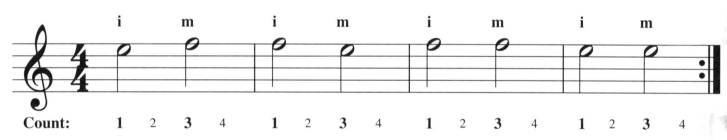

 8   Magnificent Two

How many quarter notes can fit into one half note?

_____

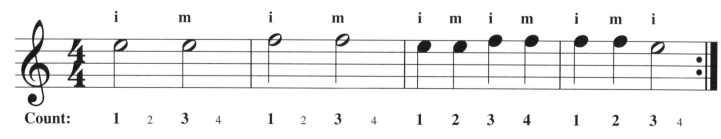

The Note G

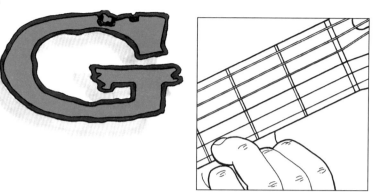

Is the note **G** in a space or on a line?

_____

Which note is higher on the staff, **G** or **F**?

_____

The Note **G** is written on top of the staff.

G Note

Play this **G** note with your **third finger** behind the **third fret** on the **first string**.

Exercise 9 uses all three notes on the first string. Clap and count before playing.

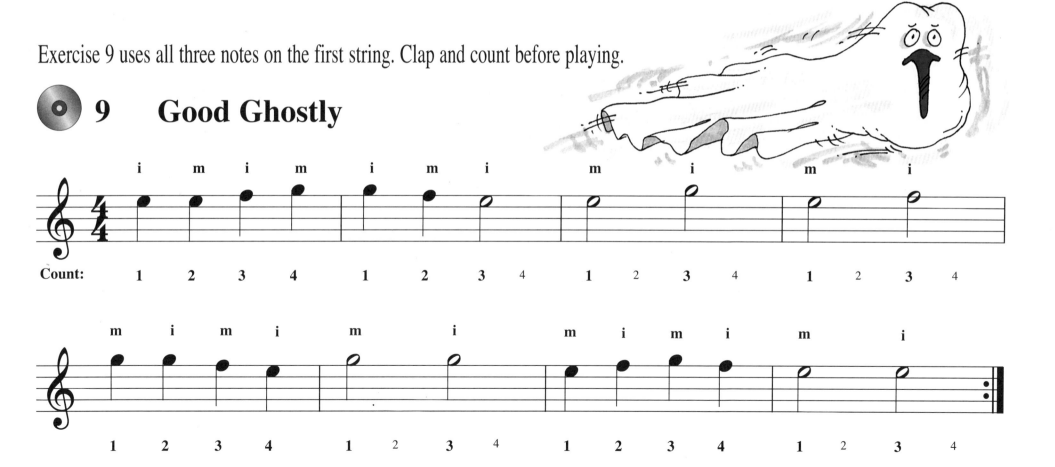

9   Good Ghostly

Lesson 4
The Note B

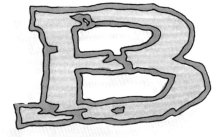

The Note **B** can have its stem going **up** or **down**.

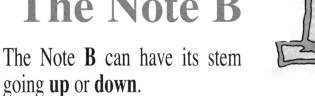

B Note

Is the note **B** in a space or on a line?

_____

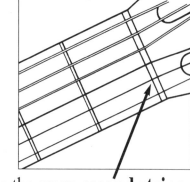

The note **B** is the **open second string**. No left hand fingers are used.

The Whole Note

Count: 1 2 3 4

This is a **whole note** (or semibreve) .
It lasts for **four** beats.
There is **one** whole note in one bar of $\frac{4}{4}$ time.

How many quarter notes can fit in a whole note?

_____

How many half notes can fit in a whole note?

_____

10 **Bee-Ware!**

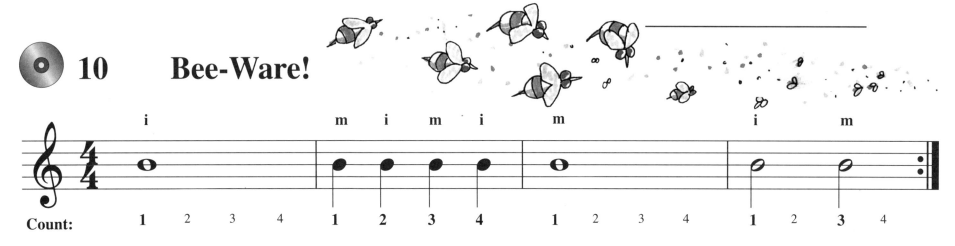

The Note C

Is the note **C** in a space or on a line?

_____

Which note is **lower, B** or **C**?

_____

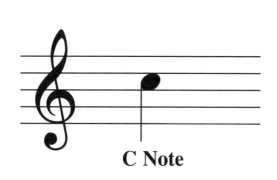

C Note

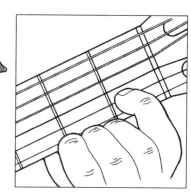

Play this **C** note with your **first finger** behind the **first fret** on the **second string**.

 11   Be Cool

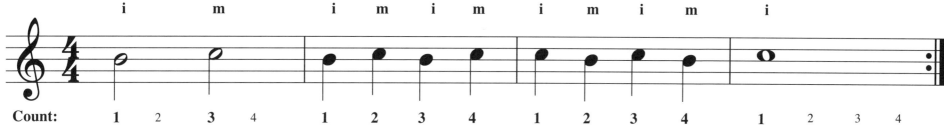

The following piece is exactly the same as the above, but played on the first string instead.

 12   Eleven Notes

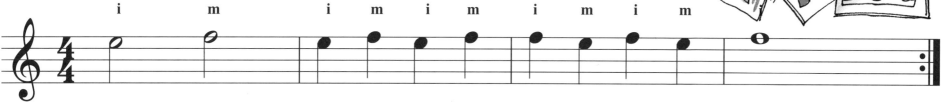

The Note D

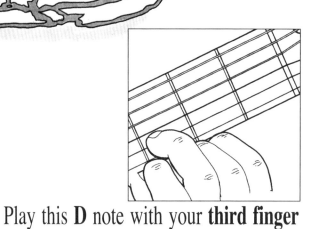

Is the note **D** in a space or on a line?

_____

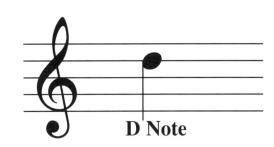

D Note

Play this **D** note with your **third finger** behind the **third fret** on the **second string**.

Follow the i-m fingerings carefully, sometimes the same finger is used twice in a row.

 13 Hot Cross Buns

m i m m i m m i m i m

Count: 1 2 3 4 1 2 3 4 1 2 3 4 1 2 3 4

 14 In the Light of the Moon

m i m i m m i m i m i

Count: 1 2 3 3 1 2 3 4 1 2 3 4 1 2 3 4

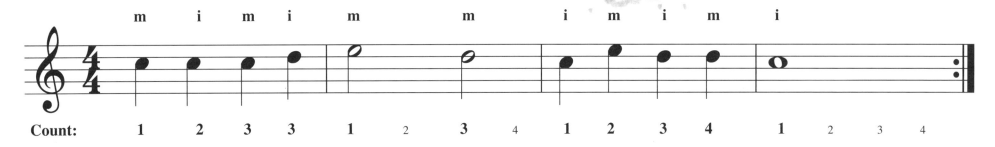

Mixing Strings 1 & 2

When using your left hand you should always make sure that the palm of your left hand runs parallel with the guitar fretboard. This means you will have to stretch the fingers apart in order to reach the correct places behind the frets. Try to hover your left hand fingers above the frets, already in place to play the next note.

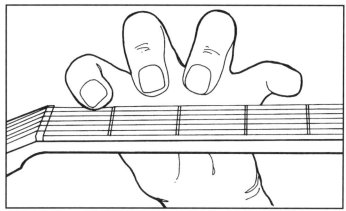

Things to remember:
1. Play a new piece slowly and evenly. Practice one bar at a time and only move on when you have mastered it evenly.
2. For the left hand use the tips of your fingers and keep the fingers curved.
3. Always count while playing.
4. Try to look at the music, not the guitar.

15   Go Tell Aunt Nancy

Go tell Aunt Nan - cy, go tell Aunt Nan - cy, go tell Aunt Nan - cy, the old grey goose is gone.

Lesson 5

The Three Four Time Signature

This is called the **three four** time signature.
There are **three** beats in each bar.
Three four time is also known as waltz time.

How many quarter notes fit in one bar of four four time?

_____

How many quarter notes fit in one bar of three four time?

_____

In the three four time the first note (beat) of the bar has a stronger feel than the other beats. Before playing the next piece, put an S for strong under every first beat and a W for weak under every other beat.

When playing, the first beat of every bar should be played slightly louder than the others.

 16   Three Four All

There are 6 beats on the recording to introduce this piece.

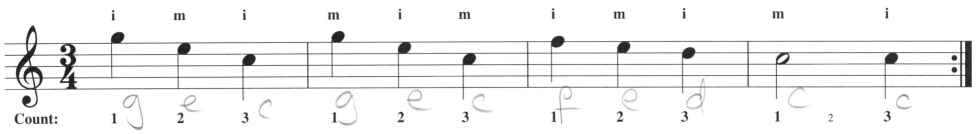

The Dotted Half Note

Count: **1** 2 3

A dot after a half note means that the note is held for **three** beats.
This is called a **dotted half note.**

How many quarter notes fit in a dotted half note?

_____

17 Dotted Waltz

Remember to play the first beat of a bar a little stronger than the others. Is your right hand thumb still resting on the top string?

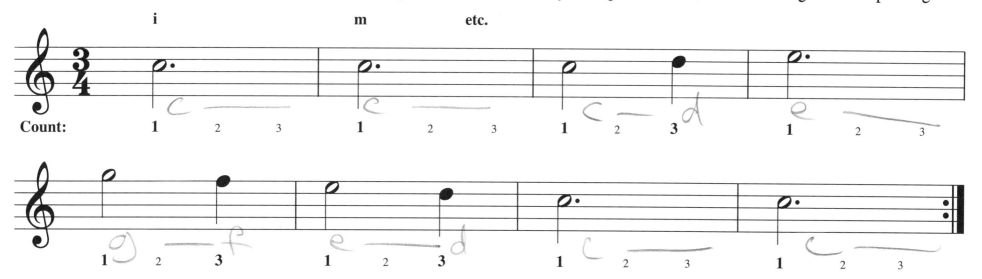

Things to remember:

1. Alternate i and m starting with i unless stated otherwise.
2. Keep the left hand fingers curved and close to the strings.
3. Count while playing.
4. Look at the music, not the guitar.

18 The Boating Song

Jacques Offenbach

This next piece was written by a composer (music writer) from the 1900s and is the first classical piece you will learn. It has no repeat sign.

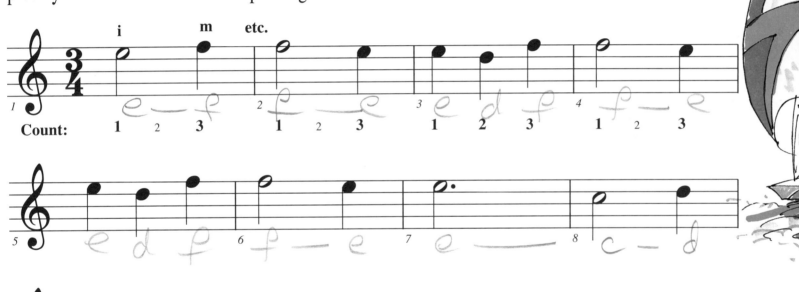

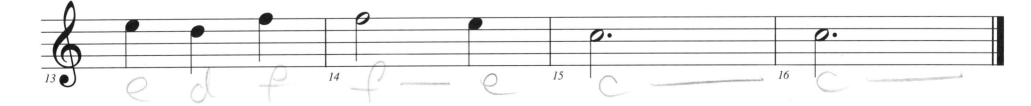

19 Ode to Joy   L. V. Beethoven

Beethoven is one of the best known composers of classical music, who lived in the 1700s. This piece is a very happy piece, as the title implies, it means a dedication to happiness. Beethoven became deaf from an illness, but still continued to compose music.

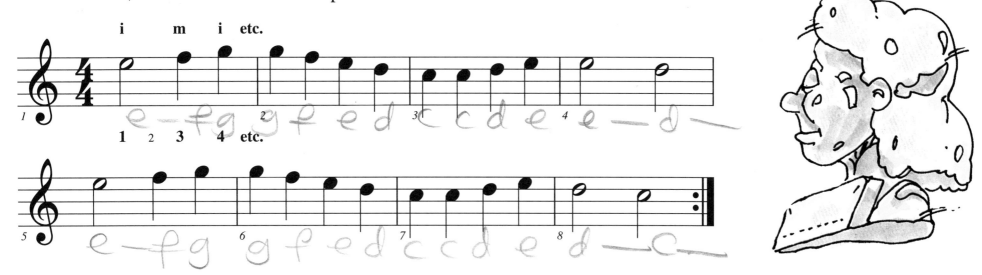

Compose your own piece using all the words from the circles below and cross each word out when used. It should be four bars long and have its own title.

B, C, D, E, F and G notes

treble clef sign

dotted half note

quarter note

half note

three four time signature

Lesson 6
The Quarter Rest

 This symbol is called a **quarter rest**.
It means there is **one beat of silence**.

Count: 1

When a rest comes after a note, that note must be stopped by lifting your finger off the fretboard, but not off the string. That is, the string is not pressed down against the fretboard. Keep counting even when you see a rest.

Count: 1

Small numbers are placed under rests.

 20 Have a Rest

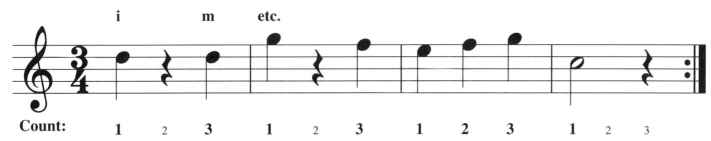

i   m   etc.

Count: 1 2 3   1 2 3   1 2 3   1 2 3

 21 Good Evening Friends

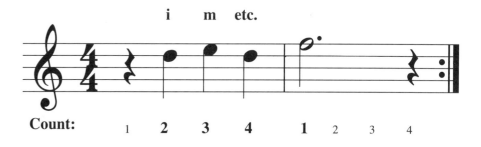

i m etc.

Count: 1 2 3 4   1 2 3 4

Ready for a Challenge?

Write the correct finger names.

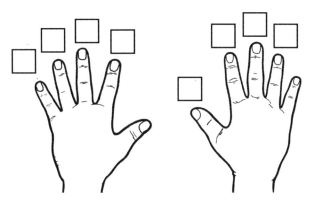

Put barlines in the correct places. There are three bars.

Write down the correct names for each note and rest. Then fill in the counts each one gets.

Write down which note is in a space or on a line by colouring the correct colour into the circle next to the letter.

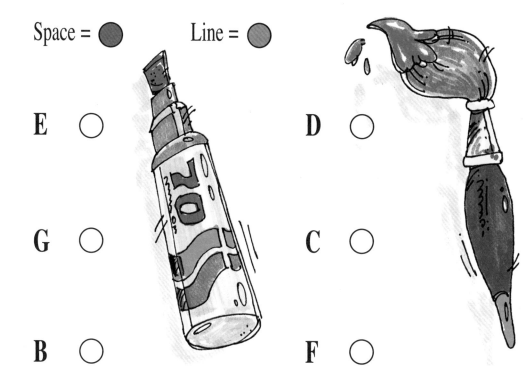

Space = ●   Line = ●

E ○   D ○

G ○   C ○

B ○   F ○

The Half Rest

This symbol is called a **half rest**.
It means there are **two beats of silence**.
This rest is written on the third line of the staff.

Count: 1 2

How many quarter rests fit in a half rest?

_____

🔘 **22 Aura Lee**

Remember to use i-m. Start the following piece with **m**.

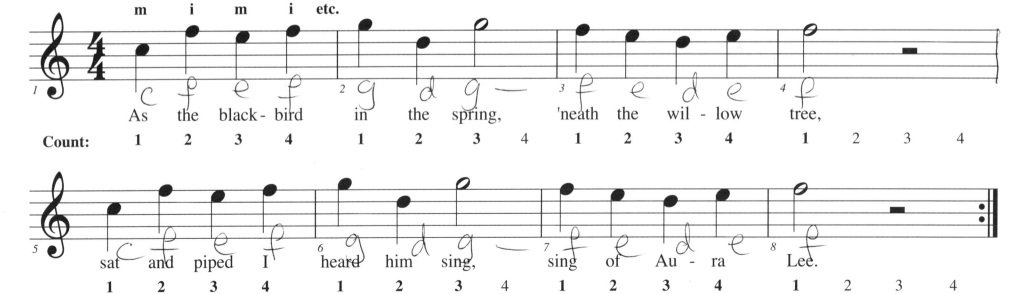

Lesson 7
The Lead-in

Sometimes a piece starts with an incomplete first bar. There may only be three beats, two beats or even one beat in the first bar. There are 5 beats on the recording to introduce this piece.

23 Take It Away!

The notes in the first bar are called **lead-in** notes or an **anacrusis** note. The missing note will always be found in the last bar of the piece, so that together they add up to one full bar. Count the missing note (or notes), but do not play it. All the pieces of Lesson 7 use the i-m alternation with the thumb of the right hand resting on the sixth string.

24 The Cuckoo

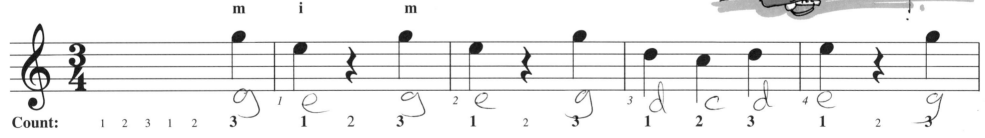

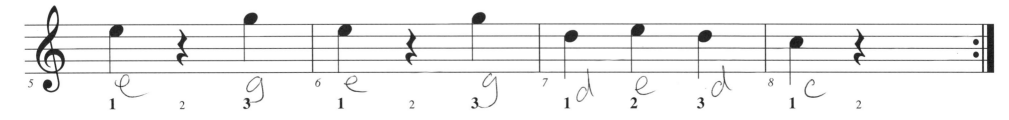

25 **The Banks of the Ohio** Traditional

26 When the Saints Go Marchin' In

Notes and Terms

Name	Quarter Note (crotchet)	Half Note (minim)	Dotted Half Note (dotted minim)	Whole Note (semibreve)
Note	♩	♩	♩.	𝅝
Rest	𝄽	𝄼	𝄼 𝄽	𝄼
Number of Counts	1	2	3	4

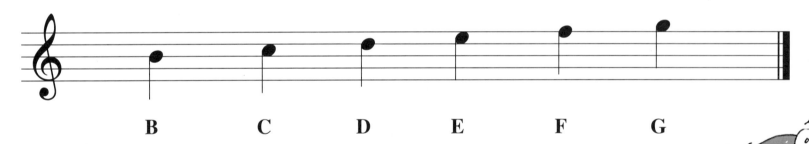

B   C   D   E   F   G

Anacrusis = Note(s) in an incomplete first bar of a piece.

Composer = Someone who writes music.

Tempo = The speed or pace of a piece.

Waltz = a piece in three four time, very often a dance piece.

Proceed to Book 2